A BLACK MANIFESTO
IN JAZZ POETRY
AND PROSE

This volume is evidence of some of the many talents of
Ted Joans, painter, poet, jazzman. Though the mood
varies from fierce pride in the Black Power Manifesto
to critical enthusiasm in Jazz Expo, to the often lyrical
perceptiveness of the poetry, there is an underlying
similarity between all three: the powerful and unbroken
rhythmic line which carries both prose and poetry forward
like a subtle musical beat. These are works to be read
aloud, to be listened to with the unrestrained ear reserved
for the best of jazz.

Ted Joans was born in Cairo, Illinois, in 1928 and studied
Fine Arts at Indiana University. He has since lived in many
parts of the world from New York to Timbuctoo. A Black
Pow-Wow of Jazz Poems was published in the United States
in 1969 and will be published in Britain in 1971.

By the same author

Funky Jazz Poems

Beat Poems

All of T.J. and No More

The Hipsters (a book of collages)

The Truth

Afrodisia

A Black Pow Wow of Jazz Poems

SIGNATURE SERIES

A BLACK MANIFESTO
IN JAZZ POETRY
AND PROSE

Ted Joans

CALDER & BOYARS · LONDON

First published in Great Britain 1971
by Calder & Boyars Ltd
18 Brewer Street London W1

ISBN 0 7145 0713 X cloth edition
ISBN 0 7145 0714 8 paper edition

Printed in Great Britain by
Latimer Trend & Co Ltd
Whitstable, Kent

Dedicated
to
Charles 'Bird' Parker
and
Malcolm X

CONTENTS

PROPOSITION FOR
A BLACK POWER MANIFESTO

PROPOSITION FOR
A BLACK POWER MANIFESTO

This manifesto that I write this night
in this city where
many other revolutionary manifestos have been written
by those who cherished freedom enough to fight and win
against enslaving forces
I feel it is my duty as a black poet
to create this manifesto for my black people.

Perhaps this Black Power manifesto will serve as a guide
   book to black liberation.

The purpose of this manifesto is to provoke black men to
   take action
to instruct them to defend themselves
and to hip them to just What, Why, How, When, Who and
   Where of Black Power.

The language that this manifesto is written in is black-talk
for black-talk is our own black language (dig Dunbar,
   Hughes and Babs Gonzales).

Black-talk is Black Power too.

There is nothing in our black-talk to be ashamed of
we can be proud of our creative expressions and sounds.

There is no white man created yet to say the word 'shit'
   like black men from America.

We wreck the white man's academic grammar and find new
   ways of pronouncing words.

Thus we are at all times creatively speaking
just as jazz men (our greatest black creators) create on
     their instruments.

We can talk-black, dance-black, walk-black, sing-black
and with the aid of this manifesto
I hope we can get together as Black Power
then to swing-actively-black.

To free our black selves with our own Black Power
and by any means necessary!!

Our black victory can only be won by Black Power.

That victory will be won the black way.

Black Power is our action - now!

Now ketch this shit
I believe that the moment is at hand for the black people
     to rise up
like a giant midnight ocean wave, or like a sharp fatal pain
     in the ass of racist United States
then with the swiftness of a cheetah's paw snatch our
     destinies from the ofay oppressors
Black Power can do, will do, and shall be done.

This great movement within the boundaries of the U.S.A.
     can completely disrupt, discredit, and eventually
     destroy the evil American racist system
that enslaves black people.

Black Power is the vanguard of the insurrection inside
     America today.

Black Power is our black revolutionary force of action.

Black Power is action now.

Black Power is the black people's bag.

It is a very deep and dark bag.

The Black Power bag
contains many points of view
but all aimed at serving the cause of emancipation.

Black Power is where ITS AT!

Black Power is
black people recognizing that we can achieve nothing without
    first taking (by any means necessary!) our own power
    in our black hands and do with it as we see fit.

Black Power is not an ideology of Western thought.

Black Power is spiritual unity
this unity must prevail to enable black people to wield
    themselves spontaneously into a vital force.

Black Power is the black magic of the Afro-American's
    black ancestors
the black arts of Africa's sorcerers
those who knew what to do, and when to do it, and
    how to do that!

It is the blacks that believe in their own personal strength
    to ultimately overcome
overpower
and defeat the white power system
that so-called 'invincible' capitalist empire.

Black Power can succeed.

Black unity is the key to that success.

Those cool black hustlers in the ghettos
those spooks who move like shadows
those urban guerillas that have learnt well the slum-jungle
    warfare
these beautiful black warriors can misuse, confuse, and
    abuse whitey in every large city in the U.S.A.

They can damage him and his buildings beyond repair.

The city is their battleground

13

they can take anything they want - even whitey's life
    if he gets in the way.

Black Power is the black man getting his share
collecting his back pay
from 1619 up to the present date!

The poorest blacks in the country fields and city streets
    will be the first to collect
for it is they that have remained true to Black Power.

They are those who had to know where it is at just to
    survive.

Black Power will totally change the condition of the black
    people in America. Black Power will not be used to
    make blacks become slave of blacks. Black Power is
    out to destroy enslavement. White America's system
    is built upon enslaving the black people and others of
    the Third World.

It is true that Black Power is a major revolt of a small
    minority
but it is also true that
the U.S.A. at the beginning was only thirteen small states
    that revolted against the (at that time) powerful empire
    of Great Britain

And those small states, united and won

Black Power shall win

That is crystal clear.

Black Power has a driving force of revenge. Black Power
    will retaliate any wrongs done to black people. This
    retaliation of wrongs
will be swift, sharp, and precise
like an Akan spear in a settler's back on the old Gold Coast
    of Africa.
    We gotta deal a death blow to the American white
    motherfucker!
    Black Power is that marvelous explosive mixture

which has accumulated since the first black slave
uprising - Always the same motive: FREEDOM!
Black Power shall inflict punishment upon the guilty
whites. They know who they are. Whitey can only
save himself by surrendering his only true asset:
money. Black Power wishes to change YOUR MONEY
white man. Change it from YOUR hand into OUR
black people's hands! I remember when I was a kid,
we'd sing a little ditty:

> naughts are naughts
> figures are figures
> all for the white man
> nothing for the niggers

That is one of the first things that Black Power must
rectify. White males and white females of America,
save your souls and perhaps your lives: Give up all
your money! Mail it in large sums to any black
militant organisation. Bullshit, whitey aint gonna give
up not one goddamn-penny! The white people of the
U.S.A. are the stingiest, most selfish and miserly
beings in the world. Black Power does not allow whites
to have a say in the revolution. John Browns (if there
are any!) can contribute to the struggle, but in their
own organizations. No infiltrations! Black Power is
the black people's thing. For Niggers Only!

This I state due to the fact of its sheer black beauty, its
swift dark actions, and its inevitable black victories.
These must be achieved by the black people, the so-
called Negroes, the Afro-americans, the coloureds,
the niggers; they alone must take care of the real
revolutionary business. Through Black Power, people
have come together. Through Black Power, black
people shall stay together. Black Power is strictly our
own, all black, and good.

When I say 'our', I mean just we the blacks. I am aware that
a whole lotta white motherfuckers shall buy and read
this manifesto; and some will perhaps identify with it;
but dig me whiteboy, This Ain't Your Bit!! Black Power
means liberating ourselves from the most vicious

15

system of murder and exploitation in the world. That
system is the American Way. Black Power is not a
class struggle. Black people do not have a class
system due to the consistent white Americans' racism
and black people's soulful unity. White America looks
at all black people; cotton pickers, editors, dock
workers, college graduates, statesmen etc, and they
only see a bunch of black niggers. Great for us! Thus
we the blacks are joined in Black Power eventhough
some of us may be reluctant. Also there are those
brainwashed blacks, or 'ostrich-head-individuals';
they will find themselves in a frightening no-man's
land. They being neither committed to their own
brothers of Black Power or licking the ass of white
America. Theirs is the role of the utopian
somnambulist without a dream. He can only survive
by running off to another country and observing the
revolt from there. His is the soul of a coward. He is
the living black dead. He can be brought to life again
through a shock, a black shock. Every black man of
America is needed in this revolution.

Black Power is dreams that are carried out into reality.
Black Power has the real and beyond the real in
which to move. Our African ancestry has enriched
us with this marvelous surreality. Black Power
warriors can change into invisible animals that can
spring out of the electric wiring inside of whitey's
house. The spirits and demons have always been
black. Black Power is that dream of self-determina-
tion, self evaluation, and self liberation brought into
wide awake action. Black Power shall liberate all
black people, and that liberation shall be achieved by
any means necessary. Thus it is no longer up to the
whiteboy to say what we should do
or how we should conduct our black revolution.

Black Power is black soul. Perhaps many of my black
sisters and brothers will wonder why I started this
manifesto off on a violent scream; well dig, that
violent scream is just a joyful noise to stir the black
giant. I started blowing this first chorus like Dizzy
Gillespie used to take the trumpet solo break on Night

In Tunisia. After all this manifesto is not a rhetorical Western primer for intellectuals, especially the armchair species.

This manifesto was not written to place black people deeper into the grip of white U.S.A. way of life. This manifesto is NOT for integrating blacks into that evil imperialistic system, but to dis-integrate those few token niggers to wake up the black masses and to suggest a creative black revolution.

Black people must take matters into their hands. Here are some political means by which Black Power can achieve full decision-making power for black people: ONE. not to support any white party of political machinery unless these white parties include Black Power candidates in vital positions and the white politicians are undisputed 'Uncle Johns' (i. e. white Uncle Toms). or TWO. separate from all white political parties and organize black ones. or THREE. build a new version of our black African ancestors political system, thus discarding the entire Graeco-Roman-Christian bag of tricks. We must not become the monsters that white Americans already are. We must have a political position so strong that white America would not dare (in the future) to misuse a country of the Third World. Americans would have to live in peace or die.

Black Power must have a political position so tight
so strong
and so positive
that the continents of Asia and Africa would look toward us as their true friends.

If there are amongst the black brothers those who feel Black Power should be led by some foreign political machinery or ideology, then I declare: If there existed at the time of this writing, a political party in the world which was both revolutionary and non-totalitarian, I mean one not presuming to dictate all the forms of spiritual activity, Black Power would perhaps align itself with that party. Since there is no

such party, Black Power strikes out alone, rather
than accept the stifling present day political machinery.

Black Power is not a nationalism but a 'black naturalism'.
This naturalism is based upon the natural desires of
black people. Black Power is not out to win the Civil
Rights' struggle, but to win the Human Rights'
struggle. Black Power is like jazz, it is based upon
the freedom of the spirit. That spirit is black. Black
people must never lose that freedom of spirit.

For it is that very spirit that has kept black people from
committing mass suicide in this U.S.A.

We must make our own new social forms, those natural
ones. And as I mentioned earlier, a political form
based on the many ancient African tribal laws, but
altered to suit our present day technological age.

Black Power's concern is all the black people. Black Power
must help financially and physically our brethren of
the Third World. Black people anywhere in the world
are not free until ALL BLACK PEOPLE ARE FREE!
There will be those who will say that black men of the
world cannot ever get the black unity that is needed.
But I say to those unbelievers: As long as there is
white racism, there will always be a black unity
whether one believes or not.

True there will be those that are brainwashed into
believing that they are some white nationality first
and blacks second
or that they are more 'civilised' than black Africans
or worse still, those who feel that they are just victims of
circumstances
that being black has nothing to do with their enslavement.

(Usually this type is a black bourgeois: with some money)

And they add that, we blacks never had it so good! Shit,
who are they trying to fool?

This manifesto is a 'Do-it-your-black-self-but-together'
book.

The vital force of Black Power is the willingness of black
people to unite to fight that white slave master. And
for those few blacks
that disagree with some of the methods to achieve self
liberation
that I have put forth in this manifesto
I can only wish them good luck (if they have some tough
shit of their own).

Black Power is fanatical
for freedom

Black Power preaches hate
the white oppressor

Black Power does advocate violence
To any white motherfucker that violates a black!

Black Power is black pride. Black Power is black
consciousness. Many of the blacks do not know who
they are (or do not want to be reminded)

We are strong people, we came from the best,
and we had to be of the best
to survive slavery!

We are not 'like white' American people. They can learn
to copy us but they cannot swing black, because we
are the original. Black Power seeks to transform
this U.S.A. It will place the values where they really
belong. No more white musicians getting rich from
jazz.

Black Power shall put a stop to that. Black musicians shall
reap the wealth of their vital seeds that they have sown.

Black musicians old and young
known and unknown
can have a black revolt that is unswerving but motivated
in perfect clarity.

Shit, what I mean is that black cats can 'fuck up' the next
white musician that climbs on the bandstand to imitate

a nigger and GET PAID FOR IT.

Black musicians will collect the largest amounts of money
    in the jazz music world. It is all possible, in this
    revolt to take control of every power position in the
    jazz music business. This revolt of reason itself
    against a state of things it judges evil, knows its
    evil, and aware of its guilt in its evilness.

Black music will at last pay off
to black musicians.

When those parasitic honky honkey hornblowers come
    around to steal black ideas
Black Power will deal with them. Black editors will be
    placed on all jazz magazines all over the world.
    After all, jazz is a Black Power thing. Jazz giants,
    those few black musicians that are still alive today
will be given their BACK PAY.

Every white musician that has picked the brains and stolen
    from these jazz giants will have to atone.

Black Power will not be a reign of terror
    but a way of black justice. Black Power is the people
    looking at himself for salvation. Black Power will
    see that the black people are rewarded for their work
    and contributions.

Black Power is black people charting their own destiny.
    Commanding their own culture.

Black Power is marvelous and beautiful. Black Power!
    Yeah!

Black Power will teach the blacks that Timbuctu is just
    as important to Afro-americans as Bowling Green.
    Black Power preserves that which is good in all
    black people. Black Power gives us our identity.

    With this identity established
    and with black unity
    Black Power becomes the most effective force of self
    liberation.

Black Power is well aware that blacks have slaved for
        centuries to build this U.S.A. and Black Power will
        see to it that black people will collect their BACK
        PAY.

They, the American whites OWE it
they know it
and they ARE GOING TO PAY!

Each black man with a family must be given also some
        LAND.
.

And Black Power shall see that it remains in black hands.
        Black people shall not live in misery,
filth
and danger.

Black Power will transform the ghettos into black
        metropolises
        that will be places of black pride in urban achievement.
        Black Power shall see to it that all the business
buildings and schools are black owned and black run.
I think you dig me, that it is crystal clear
that Black Power is out to get whitey OUT of the black
        scene forever.

Black Power's deeds are noble. Black Power is when a
        black man is pro-black. This does not automatically
        make a black man anti-white. Because it is not the
        philosophy of Black Power to hate a white man for
        his lack of color. Black Power advocates the adoration
        of being black.

Black Power is out to destroy the oppressive white system
        that enslaves the people of the Third World. They, the
        white power structure have tried to keep all the non-
        white people apart
by controlling the mass media
propaganda into infinity
and paid puppets or tokenism.

But white man has failed due to white U.S.A.'s white
        blatant, uncontrolled racism. Black Power is in the

21

position to change that evil white American system.
Black Power is not interested in whitey coming forth
to confess his guilt
no baby!

We want him to open up his godamned bank to us
remove his military out of the lands of the Third World
(who appointed him sheriff of the World anyway?).

Black people are no longer patient
ño longer praying

and Black Power cannot tolerate the American system that
prevails today. There is no place to run and hide
Niggers are ALL OVER AMERICA!! Remember my black
brothers
we are no longer that Twenty Million that they have
been reporting for the last ten years. Black people
like to fuck
and have babies
so how could we still be that same number of people that
we were ten years ago.

Our black African family heritage is a 'togetherness'. We
must have this solidarity at all levels to win our
independence from white men.

Thus it will avoid becoming a doctrine of constituted
defensive laws
and contradictory to black people's spirit. We do not need
the white man's academic bullshit
that is HIS hang up. To box in a good thing like Black Power
would be to kill it
or make it square.

Black Power is dignity, a human dignity for black people.
Black Power makes it alright for the black to be the
best in the West.

Black Power is when all black people are self-sufficient.
Man, oh man! we have gotta git the bread!! And we
are going to COLLECT that bread
for all the DUES that our forefathers and mothers had to

pay
and collect also for the dues that we are paying NOW! This
    is not just for the individual
but money for all the blacks.

Black Power is NOT a reverse racism. Black Power is not
    the same as white power. Black Power is NOT a
    temporary phenomenon. The only poor people that
    Black Power is concerned with are poor black people
    of America, first and foremost. We must first take
    care of our black scene at home
then we can grow stronger. Black people's contribution to
    the Third World is our vanguard revolution inside the
    boundaries of America. We are in the most strategic
    position. We must not desert these vital posts
by moving into one single area
where the heinous American military could do us IN
like waste us in one blow.

Naw baby, let's stay scattered
yet together in small groups. They cannot drop a bomb on
    us as long as we are right next to their best friends
    and relatives.

Whitey is cruel and dumb
but he aint that stupid.

Each group of black people will be a Black Power base
    holding as much power importance as Harlem
which whitey will always look upon as Black Power
    headquarters. We can keep in touch with our leaders
    through spiritual means, you dig?

Black Power is not concerned with the black man's beliefs
    or dogma
be he Christian
Muslim
or Buddhist
everything is okay
although Black Power's aim is the total liberation of
    black people from Western hang-ups.

Black Power is a fierce black hope. Black Power is

determined to surmount all obstacles. Black Power
does not encourage non-violence when facing the white
power system's zombies. Black power equates the
non-violent tactics with simple suicide.

Whitey is a vicious, cruel, and very violent oppressor
the American species is one of the worst. Black Power
    can and through black unity shall prevent America's
genocide of the black people. Black Power is life
giving force to black people.

Black Power shatters the integration myth. That myth was
    promised to niggers so long
that even those few that believed it was possible
finally forgot it
it was only a white power subterfuge. The white power
    system's concept of integration (even though a myth)
    was assimilation like the French and Belgian
    colonialist tried in old Africa. This assimilation
    assumes that a black man has nothing to offer the
    world
or that what is black is ipso facto inferior.

Integration meant the degradation of black people.

It meant giving up all that is great in black human beings.

It meant for all blacks to deny their Black Power. Many
    blacks were guilty of trying to even look like whitey
by committing violent acts upon their physique
such as straightening their natural kinky hair
bleaching their skin
etc...

Whitey made it clear to black people that it was
a drag to be born black in America.
He goofed by not accepting those few niggers that wanted
    to imitate him by denouncing black values. He goofed
    real bad when he said that America was the Home of
    the Brave
Land of the Free
etc., bullshit! bullshit! bullshit! Yeah whitey goofed.

The total demystification of the white man and his history
is one of the ultimate tasks for Black Power. His white
ways and means
white facts and figures
white aesthetics and cultures
all of it has been hung like a yoke around the necks of black
men.

The best white man upon the earth today is really the
worst one: the American white. All the white men
look up to
or imitate to some degree
that overgrown white boy-girl. Europeans either envy or
look with pride at the American whites. They feel that
they owe their very life to the 'liberating American
military'
who saved them from disaster. They forget that the
American whites are the worst whites upon the face of
the earth
due to the fact that
they are the descendants of
the criminals, prostitutes, whores, murderers, thieves,
mad men, insane women, religious nuts, tramps, etc.
those vile creatures who were kicked out of Europe or sent
to the Red men's country to kill and plunder. But
white men in Europe have joined hands with America
and her politics of neo-imperialism which have
replaced Europe's old styled colonialism. Europeans,
with the exception of a few individual intellectuals, give
nothing but lip service to express their dislike for
America's overt racism. Not one white country has
threatened to break off diplomatic relationship with the
United States. The European has not yet realized that
Black Power is a part of the international struggle of
oppressed people; and that it works indirectly towards
freeing them also from America's dictatorial grip.
Some are even opposed to Black Power. Even though
millions of white Europeans are being exploited, they
still look up to white America as being their leader.
And too, some of the European countries and systems
are almost as racist in nature as the United States.
There aint really no green pastures in Europe.

Especially when it comes to green backs
big bread
and some power. There are black people
that have been over on this side
since only god knows when
and they still aint got enough power to throw
some black weight around. Most of them are still in the
　　rat race trying to make ends meet. So black people
　　cannot look to Europe for a fruitful revenge.

I grant you that the white man has many technical (all can
　　be taught and learned) facilities. But where is the
　　white man when without the technical jive and strong
　　money? Then he aint shit! Take his machine science
money away and HE IS FINISHED! Clark Kent the comic
　　strip character alias Superman
is the average white man's dream of himself. Some even
　　feel that they <u>are</u> the Superman. If they <u>are</u> Supermen
why dont they outrun the black man
out box the black man
out jump the black man
out basket ball the black man
out baseball the black man
out football the black man
Fuck and out point the black man?

Afterall it was the whitemen that created some of these
　　sports, their rules and regulations

The reason is
that the white man is so caught up in his own superman
　　myth image
that he cannot humanly overcome such a personal confron-
　　tation. His sick ego drives him into believing that he
　　is still the best even though he loses. If the truth is
　　ever presented through all the means of the mass
　　media
it would show
that more than half of the so-called 'inventions' and
　　'discoveries' made (supposedly) by white men
were actually created by non-whites.

Black Power is when black people are turned onto the

26

long suppressed historical facts concerning black men and women. Black Power is black people being ready (and staying ready!) to do the hard work for Freedom.

We shall no longer be unsung heroes
our roar will
shatter the lies
black rose petals shall
come crashing into the
hearts of the world.

Jazz music is our natural
black anthem
the blues. Bessie Smith means more to black people than
    Betsy Ross. Our black music didnt just begin with the
    great Buddy Bolden
nor did it end with Ornette Coleman. It is eternal and
    strong. Africa is all over it
under it
inside of it
and thus protects it. It is a living art
a basic human need
filled with goodness
and beauty. For the non-white there is a future, for our
    socialist
creations are alive and warm. Burn baby burn! Squirm
    whitey squirm!

The black resistance movement must escalate beyond mere
    bottles and bricks. Guns! Guns can still be had
even though at the time of this writing they (white officials)
    are trying to pass a law to outlaw weapons to private
    citizens. Guns! We, black people need weapons for
    self defense.
There will be no more lynchings
when we all got guns to cut the lynch mob down.

Guns! The fuzz will think twice before he police whips a
    nigger
when the entire ghetto is armed.
Guns are good for good black folks to defend their homes
    and family.

The choice of weapon
is up to you
but I would suggest
that a rifle is a revolutionary's best friend.

Pistols can be packed by black women. Pistol packing
     mammies
don't ever lay that pistol down!

Study everything about your gun
learn what it can do
and how to do it. If you do not have a gun manual
consult one of your local black ex-G.I.s.

If guns can not be obtained
one must not despair
for there are always the old reliable
African weapons
such as the bow & arrows (with or without poison), spears,
     etc.
although crude
these weapons can still kill. And they are silent.

A razor
switchblade
dagger
icepick
etc. can all be put to good use
as they have in the past. There is no weapon that cannot
     be used against 'whitey'!

Our warriors
our black warriors are the sons of warriors
ancient African men of fire and thunder
black men who destroyed the first whites that came to
     their continent to plunder. Who are our warriors
     today?

They can come from all walks of life
blackmen that may belong to several kinds of organizations
even black churches! (Onward Christian soldiers!!)
Black women that are employed in the homes and businesses
     of our white enemies

your task is to learn everything there is of interest to
Black Power concerning whitey. Check out his and her
private life
maybe it can be useful for blackmail. Your mission is to
spy and to supply information. Deception is your
stick. Whitey must be snowed under by your polite
semi-Aunt Jemima come-ons. Do not tell him the truth
unless it is necessary
and not detrimental to our resistance movement. Dont
school 'im but fool 'im! Learn baby learn! If there are
other blacks employed where you work
avoid congregating with each other
unless its for the purpose of a put-on before whitey. Whitey
must be convinced that you ARE different from the
other blacks.

Freedom fighters playing the role as an old under-paid
black janitor are just as important as the role playing
the highly-paid black executives.
They are both committed to Black Power. We must use
every means to win this war. When the word is given
all the blacks will be ready. I could write here
in detail
about what to do
when to do
and even the HOW to do
and of course the thing that every black man knows
the Where and to Whom
But NO! It is NOT good tactics to tell one's plans
in full detail
in a book such as this manifesto
where the enemy could dig it. So this manifesto cannot
instruct certain black tactics. There will have to be
a (secret) second manifesto
presented and printed by blacks only. But for the time being
this first Black Power manifesto will suffice. The time
of shouting verbal (loud) deprecations against whitey
is over. Let's be calculated and killer cool. Let's
strike like lightening
instead of roaring like thunder. If there must be a noise
let it be the drums
talking drums
war drums

black voice drums. Now is the time for Black Power
    action. That first step of action is getting our own
    black selves together. Black unity is the first rule of
    Black Power. Let the words SOUL BROTHERS AND
    SISTERS mean just that. Because our black color has
    been used by the white oppressor to misuse
abuse
and to confuse us
we the people of color must use it as Black Power to
    liberate us. We do not have to really pledge allegiance
    to the flag
it is a white symbol
a symbol of the oppressive capitalist society
Black Power is hip to what America has of value
afterall black people's blood and sweat help to make
    America rich
thus we aint gonna throw out the diamond with the dung.

Black Power is a black truth
a soul thing. We blacks have gone beyond the stage of
    explaining what soul is. We all know that soul dont
    mean a thing if it aint got that swing. Black Power
    swings!

This black truth seems most of the time too crude
and too potent
for the shy
conventional-ridden
and brainwashed
blacks to bear
Those few that suppress their black instinct can be brought
    back into the black family
by showing them that Black Power is going ALL THE WAY
and to inevitably win.

We do not want peace from America's racism.

We want to defeat America's racism.

Once we defeat America's racism

The rest of the racist systems in the world will collapse.

America is the last and largest stronghold of white racism.

We must work black to black together.

Black expectations always influence black achievement.

In conclusion I manifest that, the bit is: Black Unity!
Help each other. Protect each other. Turn each other on to
what is happening. Make each black man, woman, and
child feel that he is an important member of humanity. Let
them know that all black people are supposed to be soul
people. Make every black human proud of being born black.
Create a good feeling of racial solidarity in black
communities.

I manifest: that black people should not steal from black
businesses or black homes. If you must steal, then you
should do so from white businesses and white homes. And
too, you must not get caught. The moral of the act is that
one cannot be really 'stealing' from a white American
since the white American has already stolen that which he
owns. If you must do physical hurt, then do so to a white
person, or to his Uncle Thomases. If you are angry at
your black brother or sister, you should try to cool it.
Retire to a more tranquil surrounding for a while.

All black adults must assume responsibility for all poor
black children. Their welfare depends upon the black
adults of the black community. Black Power's future is in
their hands. We must teach them about Africa and the
black people. We must demystify the European history and
tell them 'like-it-damn-show-is' about America. Let's
make their life an easier trip by seeing to it that they are
hip!

I manifest that we must share. We the black people must
share that which we can spare. Give to the needy and the
less fortunate. If you are a musician, painter, or ex-

soldier, give lessons in your trade to the black community. Give not only to the blacks of the U.S.A., give also to the Africans. Welcome all African students to your homes and clubs. If they have been brainwashed by white America, try to make them well. Support those militant black warriors that are still fighting to liberate their countries. Help to liberate South Africa by attacking their connections and businesses located in America. Back the truly independent African countries. If you have a skill that can contribute to the economics, education, and health of Africa, then you should go and grow there. The truly independent black countries need your skill and knowledge. They will welcome dedicated black Americans. Those that are just jiving had better stay in America. But all black people should visit Africa! It is really like a big black beautiful woman, spread out naked in the sun. Her legs wide apart, arms reaching up toward the clear blue sky, and her face is covered with a big bright welcome home smile. Yeah that is what Africa is to a black man. Africa is mother. A black mother that gave birth to all the black sons and daughters in the world. Africa is our Black Power.

I manifest that it is important that we black people build good relationships with people of the Third World. We must know our true allies and they must know about us. Black Power is part of the Third World Power. We are all joined in a 'united liberation front' to rid the world of white racism and imperialism.

I manifest that we the black people must not run wild in uncontrolled rage in the street each summer. The white press and news media await our black happenings as though they are scheduled. Each summer they make millions of marks, francs, pounds and dollars reporting their distorted stories about us and our 'race rioting'. The hired murderers (the fuzz) have added new weapons to the already over-stocked arsenal. They provoke the black community. Screaming, protesting, and throwing a brick in the streets at fuzz and whitey is not where its at. Uh-uh baby, that kind of manifestation is just what the fuzz wants you to do, so that he can have an alibi (as if he needed one!) to kill black me or you. We must have creative

33

constructive destruction. We must not be blind with rage
and play into whitey's ambush. For that kind of action is
exactly like brother Muhammed (Cassius Clay) Ali
described: "like a bull running and charging a freight train".
Creative constructive destruction depends upon the wants
of the black community. Targets should be chosen months
in advance. Plans should depend more upon spontaneity.
Leaders should always be cool and firm. They should never
tell a black brother to do something that they would not do
themselves. I manifest that I am ready
to carry this
all my manifestations
out into reality if need be.

  Since this is a piece of prose
Black Power prose
a proposal for a Black Power manifesto
and not really 'the' manfesto
I wont be mad if a black cat cops-out on what I manifest.
So I continue to manifest that we must be cool, eventhough
there is a 'long hot summer'. Guerilla against the gorilla.
Black revolutionaries must teach urban revolutionary
methods to black folks. Rebellion yes, rioting no! We
must remain ready to act in our revolution at all times.
For a moment will come when passion has infected the air,
things will be tense and uptight: the black community will
be so mad that it can barely breathe, and it is then that the
most extraordinary events happen independently of any of
the preparations which have been made. But these
happenings must be done effectively. The pent-up emotions
must explode in the right directions. Do not forget that
there is no food in your home. Do not forget that your
family is as raggidy as a scarecrow. Do not forget that you
or your black brother lives above those pawnshops,
liquor shops, all robbers shops.

  I manifest that police stations, post offices, banks,
subway stations, city official agencies should be burnt,
first and foremost. It is crystal clear that we all hate
those rotten stinking, rat infested fire traps that black
people are forced to live in and pay rent for; yet when we
burn one of them crumbling brick shacks down, we often
make many black families homeless. That we must remedy.

34

It can be done by Black Power group planning. So that when the emergency arrives, everyone that is burnt out will already know where to go. Black unity is the way. Summertime, when the living is easy (for the whites!). Fish are jumping (for the whites, it is they that can afford to go on vacations!), and the cotton is high (change the word cotton to prices and there is where we the blacks come in). Well your daddy is rich (American whites only!) and your mammy is good-looking. Yeah our black mammy is good-looking, in fact she is beautiful. And each day she is growing more beautiful as we embrace Black Power. Summertime must be only their popular time to report that 'the natives are restless'. We must carry on our revolution <u>all-the-time</u>, not just in summertime.
D.D.D.V.!
Disrupt the economy.
Deceive the authorities.
Destroy the stolen properties of the enslavers of humanity.
Violently confront the racist white American.
Wherever you encounter him in the world, let him know that there is no escape. He is guilty and must pay. We blacks must revenge the atrocities of the slave trade of yesteryears, and the institutionalized racism of the present day. We must <u>not</u> forget!

I manifest that non-violence is a failure because the United States of America is not a non-violent place. White Americans are taught to be violent racists. Just dig their history books, mass media messages, and 'all-amerikkkan-way-of-life. It is he that violently opposed those civil rights bills. It is he that has systematically intimidated and killed black people when they tried to live by <u>his</u> U.S.A. Constitution. We of Black Power are not concerned with those 'silly rites' (Civil-Rights), we are concerned with Human Rights. Why should not black people be free to have their own power and live in all human liberty?

I manifest that America never was a democracy. If there is ever going to be democracy, a social democracy, then white people will have to give up all their stolen wealth and it be redistributed. American Indians would have to be made rich, since this land is really theirs. Black

Power with the help of the Third World can create a new
nation out of America. It must first be destroyed, not
physically, (at least not all of it) but mentally, and
materialistically. It will not be easy. The American
military-industrial monster cannot be killed so easy. It is
strong and well entrenched. We all must be ready to
fight to win. We can win, we will win, and we are winning.
It is not the end for us, it is the beginning. Black Power
is an 'our' thing, and we must do our work to win together.

JAZZ EXPO '67

JAZZ EXPO '67

THE NEWPORT JAZZ FESTIVAL IN EUROPE

Tuesday Oct. 24th

Nightime jazztime in Londontown - Odeon Hammersmith
   Rank Theatre end of the line Underground ride - Come
   to see the three oldtimers of the tenor saxophone -
   three black B's bringing music oversea - Budd, Ben
   & Buddy.

also another black B - Bill Coleman him trumpetman -
   Budd Johnson happened first - blew straight but
   modern plus on Lester Leaps In 'great' - M.C.
   Higgins announced bad news: no Teddy Wilson, no
   Albert Nicholas tonight! - moans, groans and Oh No's
   from audience - British group backed the three black
   B's as well as playing a few numbers of their own -
   audience mostly dark suited business men and well
   dressed collegiate types - solid all white not a Third
   World face in sight - audience sitting stiff, with
   crossed legs, and tapping their manicured fingers
   rhythmically on their fat & skinny knees - Bill
   Coleman no relation musically or familywise to
   Ornette toots a bad choice of tunes and sings them yet!
   Black eye to black cats

Bill should know better! Ben Webster from Ellingtonia
   enters - wit and hipness - takes care of business in
   spite of non-support from British rick-E-tick tick
   trio behind him - Ben is boss on ballads - breathing
   hot blue flames down the horn.
Applause explodes - like thunder after Ben, the true Big
   Ben Webster finished - night air filled with traditional
   jazz sounds is disrupted - Bill Evans has been chosen

39

to replace Teddy Wilson - are they kidding? - Nope, there he blows with his trio - modern impressionist jazz pianist Bill Evans - white urban skyscraper wide street concrete park soul pouring forth - Thank god there is a Mose Allison! - Eddie Gomez the bassman plays Spic and Span bass solos - the Odeon is filled with Evans perfumery - a few businessmen getting a bit horny - some turning 'gay' - finally as quiet as they came on they float off like three feathers or three coins drowned in the perfume fountain - Next Newport All Stars - and who is that on piano? Is it Pere Ubu? bleached Fats Waller? the waiter from Katz's Delicatessen? Naw, all wrong - It is George Wein the cat who started the whole Newport Jazz Festival scene - Yep he is sitting there and having a ball - with Don Lamond drums

Jack Lesberg bass

Ruby Braff (who made me laugh to hear trying to blow nigger on I want a Lil' Girl)

and the other black B: Mr. Buddy Tate - he remembered me from 1946 - Buddy is an ex-Count Basie tenorman and was in that blasting swinger band when I was a teenager and worked backstage as a bandboy - Buddy dug into a Prez bag for some reason this night - everything was all right on I Want a Lil' Girl

Buddy was all black Buddy - George Wein supported the scene - he soloed well on Honeysuckle Rose - proving that sometimes being around great jazz music and musicians will rub off on you - more bounce to the pound & ounce in Wein's piano playing though

Wednesday Oct. 25th

Jazztime again time - late start time Roland Kirk time - Kirk sharp in his shiney black space suit - Whats It All About tune is brutally beautiful blown by multi instrument blind musician Kirk - Ellington's Creole Love Call interpreted by Roland blowing clarinet &

tenorsax simultaneous - big black jazz mouth of Kirk - breathing out of his pores thus using other openings for musical instruments - Bosch predicted there would be a Roland Kirk - audience doesnt get the messages that Kirk often expresses during his solos - they sit, cold, stiff and unrelaxed - but explode with loud applause after each number is finished - is it to be polite? - Kirk is the bravest breather in jazz - taking long winded chances - he is 'for real plus all soul' - flute solo interspersed with African chants & field hollers - blowing out of his nose with some toy - leaping into classic flute style just to show whitey that he can - doing Tribute to Trane switching back and forth from alto, soprano and tenor - jess fer kicks doing a bagpipe bit in jazz style - Great jazz Great Roland Kirk set - Intermission - audience is conditioned to good sounds with heat - Charles Lloyd Quartet comes on dressed in Flower Folk fashion - Lloyd is a drag - he is a black Brubeck on saxophone - He tried every trick in the trade and failed - all tunes un-announced - Charles Lloyd's honest soul can be weighed by the ounce! - Keith Jarrett took care of business along with Jack DeJohnette - the pianist and drummer - Lloyd on flute sounded like a young middle class white boy on his first jazz gig - the audience was not to be fooled they knew he was jiving instead of jazzing - they froze on him - weak applause - polite courteous audience -

As a musician Lloyd flopped as a black cat he is making history - in black infamy - I compare Charles Lloyd to the black pig of the Congo: Tshombe - both traitors and sell outs -

The U.S. government sent Lloyd to Russia but wouldn't dare send a true avant-garde group like Ornette Coleman, Archie Shepp, Albert Ayler etc...

Unhip whitey will wake up someday and find out about their Uncle Thomas of jazz.

Thursday Oct. 26th

Nightime rightime jazz time theatre marquee reads:
 American Folk Blues Festival - it should have read
 (since there were no Hillbillies, Okies, Dave Van
 Ronks, etc) Black American Folk Blues Festival or
 Afroamerican Folk Blues Festival - audience young
 healthy looking folkniks and upper bohemians over
 thirty - Bukka White with steel guitar alone on stage
 representing me and all U.S.A. blacks - voicing for
 30 million NICE colored people - masculine with
 heavy down home dialect - Memphis style git-tar
 strumming - coon can gestures - reminds me of my
 illiterate uncle who blew git-box when I was four and
 collected coins for him - Aberdeen Blues a master-
 piece of Black Power!!!
Chicago group fronted by Lil' Walter who is a folknik
 favorite - Lil' Walt in his green sweater and pegged
 trousers blew his harmonica in his well known style
 - Mississippi Son House brought down the house -
Old black cats of black music never really age - their
 music keeps them alive and makes us all grow younger
 and hipper - Skip James, Hound Dog Taylor, Odie
 Payne, Dillard Crume were all 'good men, you can
 understand' (quoted from Skip James' Washington D.C.
 Hospital Blues) but Koko Taylor, a Bessie Smith
 shouting wailer, that only put-on a whitey accent to
 announce her tunes - sexually she turned all the men
 in the crowded auditorium on with her Rock Me Daddy
 Roll Me Until I Want No More (translation: Fuck me
 lover, fuck me until I want no more) Brownie McGhee
 and Sonny Terry came on - no one had to worry - they
 cooked! a black club foot & black blind man made more
 musical sense in all honesty than whitey had ever
 dreamed of -
These two men are geniuses - Brownie McGhee guitarist
 and Sonny Terry harmonica player - both singers &
 natural swingers - Sonny sometimes blows Coltrane-
 like phrases or does phrases like Charlie Parker

Perhaps I should reverse that statement - Yeah I meant it
 the other way around - Afterall he is black daddy of
 them - To witness these two giants wail on that stage

before an almost completely white audience makes me
as a black cat feel so proud that I could explode in sheer
joy
What a pair of truths!
Went home filled with ecstatic black consciousness - up
lifted - with hope - and love - I'd heard the message!

Friday Oct. 27th

Again Jazztime nightime - Herbie Mann and his all black
group - Vibist Roy Ayers playing well out of Milt
Jackson's deep bag - Herbie with a weak flute tone plus
over long solo -
But Herbie did inspire the group at times -
The experience of the night for me - guitarist Sonny
Sharrock - first guitarist blowing the New 'Thang'
avant-garde jazz - to describe his playing: he holds his
guitar straight in front of him vertical

he rakes across the strings at times
he doesn't play rhythm with the section
he lays out as though he was a trumpet or saxophone -

He sounds a bit like Albert Ayler and yet...
He is unlike anything I have ever heard - too bad Herbie
didnt give him more space to solo - he told me he
just cut an album with Pharoah Saunders -
Man I cant wait to dig that - Sonny Sharrock is black -
Afroamerican like all the other avant-garde mothers
of value - he is an innovator -
Whitey will watch him, copy him and perhaps get rich
performing his music - that is the plight of the black
jazz innovator. Herbie Mann closed the set with an
AfroCuban version of a John Lennon tune.

Intermission standees who paid only five shillings stood
three deep - more young folks but still cannot see any
hippies - perhaps they change clothing when they dig
jazz - more blacks & browns at this concert - more
beards too.
Monk! Thelonious SPHERE Monk - the surrealist of
modern jazz - the Dadaist of traditional piano playing
- Ruby My Dear first tune - Charlie Rouse not in good

form - having difficulty with his tenorsax reed - Monk
leaves piano takes an elegant stroll around the stage -
stands in the far left corner - in the shadows digging
the group - returns takes out the tune - Quartet starts
tune augmented now by Ray Copeland - Ray blowing
Dizzy trumpet style - flugel & trumpet horns - Monk
split from piano hurriedly - rushes around the stage
and off and back again - mystery sweeps the audience
- Monk whispers to the playing musicians - they whisper
back - Monk left alone on stage - Dont Blame Me piano
solo by His Hipness - surrealized truths -
Jimmy Cleveland trombonist
Phil Woods alto sax
Johnny Griffin tenor sax augment the group -

Well You Neednt
Strong sound - all Monk - Griffin solos - holds his
horn in a taking a pee position - blows great tuff-tenor
solo -
Mysteriosa a Monk tune built on the chords of Whitey's
Just Me, Just You standard ballad - Griffin is a Ray
Charles of the tenorsax - a preacher - Jimmy Cleve-
land gets one solo - not too exciting - but Phil Woods
takes advantage of his one solo spot -
Takes a hell of a wailing alto sax solo - marred at times
by his Bird & Cannonball borrowing - Clark Terry
comes on with his trumpet and plunger - Blue Monk -
Fine trumpet - excellent Monk pianistics - Monk is still a
genius - he is still The Loneliest Monk in the world
of music - Great sounds -

Saturday Oct. 28th

Arrived late I did - Jim Hall blowing his cool blue flame
throwing guitar - sophisticated and beautiful - white
but right!! Hall is in the category of white jazzmen
like Lee Konitz, Gerry Mulligan, Pee Wee Russell,
Al Haig, Stan Getz etc -
White cats like these few have their own - they are
parallel to the few black millionaires in
the U.S.A. - rare!

George Benson next guitarist - Benson bopping all over the
place - but he knows how not to turn up the amplifier -
Pop-Rock guitarists TAKE NOTE!!
The guitar workshop did work - but nothing great happened
- perhaps they should have borrowed Herbie Mann's
guitar man Sonny Sharrock -
Intermission - lots a chicks on the scene - also plenty of
the Third World Folks.
Sarah Vaughan and the Bob James trio backs her - first
song a drag - too schmaltzy, too upperclass whitey -
Sarah has always been my favorite ballad singer -
I have dug her for more than twenty five years - she is
fat now - she looks like a modern Bessie Smith - she
is so sensual - even though she was wearing a drag
shaped evening gown - on Foggy Day which she retitled
A Rainy Day in London Town she was back in the
jazz singing business - Sarah Vaughan doesnt copy
musical instruments like many other mothers do - she
uses her voice in the ways that no mechanical instru-
ment could - she is great although her choice of
material is sometimes whitey -
On Misty she was at her entertaining best
When I look at Sarah I am reminded of all those black
U.S.A. soul sisters that I have left behind and been
away from so long -
Too Long!!
Damn she sho' does look good, sound good, and bet feels
good -
The audience I feel agreed with me - Sarah's is IT!

Sunday Oct. 29th First concert

Miles and Wayne at the mike discussing on their instru-
ments - Miles Davis the quiet black volcano of explosive
truth - Wayne Shorter a smooth Trane - Herbie
Hancock pianist black impressionist - Ron Carter bass
man and Tony Williams the youngest musician in the
entire Expo '67 Festival and the best drummer -
All of Miles Davis solos this night were 'fantabulous' -
Miles blew only open horn although his harmon mute
rested on the piano - after each solo Miles like Monk
stalks around the stage sets - stands in the left

corner also - group played many of Waynes original
tunes - Miles takes breath taking astronautic solos -
blazing cadenzas - fast statements of anger - suspense-
ful
telling a story - audience is the best yet - Minister
Miles quietly turns the British jazz fans on -
Second half after intermission - Jimmy Garrison - surprise
- unannounced replacement for Charlie Haden - great
Coltrane bassist - ten minutes solo alone - joined by
Beaver drummer Harris who came to Europe last year
with Albert Ayler - Grachen Moncur III black trombo-
nist -
Rudd blows his own thing - his is a white rarity in
modern jazz - Rudd is great - finally on stage comes
Archie Shepp - attired in an African blouse and cap -
Archie stalks around like an elephant - strong tone
strong statements strong long solo - Archie Shepp is
not only a tenorsaxman but writes poetry and articles
about Third World folks - he is the ultimate of what
Black Power means - his art liberates and brings joy
- to some it scares the HELL out of them - not only
whitey but blacky too! - Archie's music is a deman-
ding music - he takes over all of one's emotions when
he blows - he never compromises -
After fifteen minutes the audience was frightened, over-
joyed, or angry - I was approached by an angry West
Indian -
He demanded that I should give him the price of his ticket
back - since I seem to enjoy that 'horrible noise' -
I ignored his brain washed or ignorant attitude - but
why did he pick me to demand money from? - Archie
and his group built up their sound like Coltrane's
Meditation or Ascension - black wave after black
waves of sound poured forth from the stage - the
audience couldn't escape - they were drowning in
sound - those like myself were caught up in the
pleasure - the spiritual rejoicing - Archie Shepp's
group destroyed all that the British jazz establishment
has thought that jazz was - they brought home the
truth that: whitey does not really KNOW his niggers -
they think that they KNOW what niggers are up to -
Archie Shepp's impact on the audience was similar to
Stokely Carmichael's impact on the London audience

46

at the Roundhouse last summer

Freedom! Freedom! Now! Now! - I could hear the music
saying - I am free!

After forty five minutes of continuous marvellous conjuring
the group broke into a popular ballad The Shadow of
Your Smile - played sly, cunningly and with guerilla
like deception - audience, after being scared shitless,
welcomes the breath-of-air let-up - But Archie resumes
the attack upon their preconceived ideas of 'knowing
where its AT' - Archie's tenor is like an elephant
trunk - roaring like a lion - or the A-Train in Harlem's
belly - many whites cannot take any more - pale, red,
and disturbed faces rush out of the auditorium -
someone shouts: Go Home! to Archie's group - that's
just it Archie Shepp's music is home - it is like the
blackman in the U.S.A. today - the poor blackman -
the blackman like me!
Archie Shepp finished the set off by falling into a circus
tune - just to remind whitey what he thought of their
musical taste - whitey of course ate this portion of
jivery up - with that bit done Archie's group left the
stage with the audience shouting for more and some
unhip ones yelling boo's -
Backstage everyone was congratulating Archie's group -
photographers took pictures and true diggers of jazz
asked for autographs - Roswell Rudd is white and
right - he is the John Brown of the New Black Wave -
He is right down front with the niggers - he paid his dues
and is still paying them!
A group of Africans waited to embrace and shake Archie's
hands - they felt he'd told their story - in fact he had
- he had covered the situation - with his music -
Vietnam, Detroit, Johannesburg, Sydney, Moscow,
Salisbury and too London - with blinding beauty of
black jazz music - he'd freed us and scared the
oppressors
The niggers were surely restless that night, yeah restless!

Second Concert Sunday Oct. 29th

Miles Davis group again starting - highlight Round Bout
Midnight stated by open horn Miles - followed by
Wayne only this time Round Bout Midnight is played
up tempo - Herbie Hancock playing with much more
force than last concert (perhaps Archie Shepp
influence?) - Tony is just the best young drummer
there is - he constantly steals the show - Miles blues
a masterpiece - heavy rubato tone - sharp as Swedish
razorblade is His Hipness Miles - best dressed man in
jazz

Intermission second half
Garrison again arco bass solo - joined by Beaver the eternal
pace setting drummer - steady and untiring - Rudd
comes on like a boxer - plunging, jabbing, ducking and
shoving his trombone with its bent bell -
He blew better than Grachen (and many other brothers) -
Beaver bombarding the audience with drums - Archie
falls in screaming - audience feelings hurt - insults
shouted from the audience - Archie and group ignore
them and continue doing their thing - hassles start
in the audience - police, I mean constables running
around in the back of the theatre like Keystone fuzz -
The whole scene is beautiful - every thing is marvelous -
Archie Shepp is a seer - a black seer like Maldoror-
He used the same format and closed with the circus march
ditty - the crowd is in an uproar - some have grown to
love his music - he has sorta liberated some of them
from their guilt (For the moment!) - they scream for
him to come back - but he cannot - the show is over -
but the truth lingers on - I and black others rush in
the dressing room and kiss him - thanking him and
his group.

ROTTERDAM HOLLAND DOELEN CONCERTGEBOUW
MONDAY Oct. 30th

I arrive out of breath in Holland rushing to the hall to hear
the sounds that have been so uplifting in London -
hoping that they would be just as great or greater here
in Holland - they were! fabulous Miles Davis group
played excellent and free form - Archie Shepp attired

in different African robe and cap came on stage like a
    freed black panther - he leaped at the microphone -
    his sax abused the Dutch jazz fans ears - they had
    never experienced anything like Archie Shepp's
    music in person before - they re-acted almost like the
    British but didnt walk out - they sat through it all and
    some uncool students of jazz threw paper wads and
    booed -
But Archie and the group just took care of jazz business -
    they wailed the truth -
Not since Albert Ayler's group have I witnessed the mass
    hysteria in Holland -
In the finale they gave Archie Shepp group a standing
    ovation -
He had to take a curtain call and ask them to go home -
    they wanted more - they had felt the truth - they had
    heard the beauty - had fallen under the sorcerer's
    spell - backstage I placed a black African gri-gri
    around Archie Shepp's neck - I had last placed a
    gri-gri around another sorcerer's black neck: Stokely
    Carmichael!
These blacks, these young black sorcerers tell whitey jazz
    truth - they are not leaders - they are music spokes-
    men - poets - and you know you have nothing to fear
    from the poet
        but the truth!!

POEMS

AFRICA

Africa I guard your memory
Africa you are in me
My future is your future
Your wounds are my wounds
The funky blues I cook
        are black like you - Africa
Africa my motherland
America is my fatherland
although I did not choose it to be
Africa you alone can make me free
Africa where the rhinos roam
Where I learned to swing
before America became my home
Not like a monkey but in my soul
Africa you are the rich with natural gold
Africa I live and study for thee
And through you I shall be free
Someday I'll come back and see
Land of my mothers, where a black god
        made me
My Africa, your Africa, a free continent
        to be

JAZZ IS........

dedicated to Cecil Taylor

a SCREAM/ can scare/ awake or shake one UP!!
to joy's highest pitch/ forth deep into fathoms where/ boss
bass sounds rumble/ round riffs repeat rhythms/ there.....
a SHOUT is whats/ thats about/ jive or groove/ right on
across the bridge/ work and rework them changes/ catch
this bit/ here not steady/ READY? accidently fell in
and out of those fast changing bars/ discovering and
uncovering/ dare a devil phrases/ skipping the last
measure at last minute/ plenty plenty soul stirred down in
it in it in it/ git up git up/ let up off that there clicks/
away heres what I gotta say/ forcing fierce fragments/
out side of me into machine voice/ tearing away its
mathematics of so-call so-believed and preached music/
a moan may cause tears/ reminds or just shatters/ the
mask is down on its knees/ now to disguise the non melody
in me/ out of me/ free/ glad to be/ keep in touch with
your axe/ truth streaming across the earth/ worming its
way/ out beyond the seas/ mountains/ fields/ and grave-
yard giggles/ sad at first burst/ bigger blacker blacks
to be had/ biggest barriers broken/ sound pounding is
swings/ let freedom swing one more again/ bright
explosions hammer human hang-ups dark moods massage
the guilt/ gas leak of pleasure/ marvelous images
surround/ brain tissues/ discarding manmade forbidden
issues/ these beats blending and bending/ back to black/
and forth to forward march/ beats heat increased/ to
arouse whats really there/ down inside/ soul sacks/ a
black sound/ a BLACK SOUND/ leaps/ or glides/ into the
ear/ of the digger (a listner who stirs) and like water and
air/ Jazz is.....
                         good for the soul

TO BE WHAT IS NOT TO BE

IF

WHEN

WHY
          IF
          WHAT
          WHERE
IF

WHO WAS
          THEN

          WHY

          WHEN
IF

WHERE

WHAT

IF

WHO

WERE
          THERE

          W A S

jamestown 1619
virginia 1619
the good ship jesus 1619
twenty strong black men sold 1619
not for very much 1619
by the christian dutch 1619
who still love gold 1619
stolen black diamonds 1619
afrikaaners kaffir keepers 1619
calvinist klompen (usa valet) 1619 florins
imperialist shell oil-sold out scene 1619
lowland 1619
netherland 1619
holland 1619
zwarte piet 1619
suriname no power 1619
zwarte piet noel 1619
A--aruba 1619
B--bonaire 1619
C--curacao
zwarte piet 1619
NIET MEER ZWARTE PIET! MAAR ZWARTE MACHT!!
this is 1969 not 1619!!!

BLACK NAILED FETISH PRAYER

A black curse of butterballs
A black spell of steel apple dreams
A black mental sickness that lasts long
    between their brainless legs
    rotting their Spanish priests' nostrils
    before Easter, Christmas, and All Saints' Day

I stand again before you
    this time with my angel of everything
    ready for my anything
    a surrealist soul/ sister
    a smiling beauty beyond the walls of Western <u>ways</u> and
    means

I bring her to you
    place her in your mirror eye view
    an aardvark, has she discovered through Malcolm X?
    and now, a pangolin through me and you?

I bathe her in black art's mysterious waters
    the depth is unquestionably deep
    bottled serpents of Africa
    twist like a kink from my hair as she passes
    especially with its parental praises of "saving Africa"

Black fetish, encrusted with your many
    nails, knife blades, shivs, etc
    Protect us in our quest
    remove evil obstacles in our path
    We are <u>not</u> 'Just any black men'.

EGO-SIPPI

i've leaned against the TOWER OF PISA took a piss in the
LOUVRE and laughed at BERLIN in ruins NOW i read
my poem in 'SIPPI
i've slept between the paws of the SPHINX wept with joy
at seeing the PYRAMIDS and crossed the SAHARA twice
(alone/stoned/& feeling nice)
NOW I read my poem in 'Sippi
i've lived at TIMBUCTOO/TANGIER/HARLEM/ & HAARLEM
HOLLAND too double crossed the Atlantic which i shall
rename THE AFRICAN OCEAN blue
NOW I read my poem in 'Sippi
and allyall know thats saying a lot

BANG BABY BANG

Hey policeman! Why do you carry a gun? to shoot me in the
back if I start to run... or is it because you are a frightened
man?
Do you go to bed with your woman
with your gun in your hand?
Hey policeman why do you carry a gun? to kill us off if we
don't obey to mass murder us the legal way... or is it
cause you're a uniformed criminal
and for you crime does pay?
Tell us policemen why do you all carry guns?
can't you enforce the law without a gun
are you afraid of the public, thus need one
does a gun give you power of life and death?
Okay policeman I'll carry a gun myself
I'll carry a gun to protect me from you
so when we dispute/we both will know/ exactly what
to do
Bang baby bang!

THE BLACK JAZZ SMILE

to lift up my horn & face the music
those black dots with white mathematical tails
to blow my soul through a white man's machine
& then allow white critic to tell me
what I blew
was either
Left (over)
Right (white)
or wrong (black song!)
to bare my self before an uncool scene
thus allowing millions to nourish &
steal from me
without me
receiving compensation, celebration
or fair explanation
Western World's way: EXPLOITATION
So to be a black jazz man & blowing an honest stick
(big masculine bag avoiding the faggot's trick)
is to be putdown
face the frowns
& be starved by white power's clowns
When he   the blackman smiles in jazz
look for the sadness   in his eyes

ALL WHITE ON   EUROPE SIXTY NINE   WESTERN FRONT

THERE IS SOMETHING ABOUT EVERYTHING
EVERYWHERE   IN   EUROPE
OF   BEING DEAD
OF   FAST DYING
THERE ARE   THOSE CHERISHED   TRADITIONS
RESPECTED   BY   EVERYBODY
EUROPEAN
WITHOUT   QUESTION
THEY STAND AS   TOMBSTONES
FOR   EUROPEANS
LIKE   AMERICAN   WESTERN FILMS
FOR   THEY WERE BUILT   ON BLOOD
FOR FUTURE   IMPERIALISTS TO GLORY   AND   FLOW
     ON
I   AM   SURPRISED   NOT   TO   SEE
A   GIANT   STATUE
OF   HITLER
IN PARIS   OSLO   OR DACHAU
THIS   IS   A CEMETERY CONTINENT
WHERE   THEY NOW   INTEGRATE   EVERY/THING/
     WHERE & BODY
INTO EUROPE'S   INEVITABLE
BORING SLOW
DEATH
THERE IS   SOMETHING
ABOUT   EUROPE
EVERYTHING   EUROPEAN
THAT ISNT YOUNG   OR
REVOLUTIONARY
THAT   ONE   CAN   CALL
DEATH

HAIRY WARNING

to Michael X of Britain

With your exploding East African hair
thrusting upward from your Bakota head
like hardwood rain forest trees
that European false belly boats
kidnap daily from
black Africa
With your blooming marabout beard
made of detonator's wires of Mozambique
black guerrillas as numerous as mosquitoes
deadly rendering stings
For white Portugal
Hairy mask framing face of soul
maumau and Miles Davis manners
taunting your Imperialist tormentors
here in blind white fog
of London
Hairs of hate grow grey in Britain
Where bulldogs still growls or grins
two sided pubs, two classes on train, facial doubles
Oh Michael X - my brother - the two sides
Black hairy heathens must battle
Britain is blind to your wild sad savage eyes
thus making you choke your naked white queen
that fucks you as a hip favor
'One must dig deep with a spade' - Africa
shouts - 'or the hole, will be Sir Charley's grave'!

PUBLIC WHITE PROBLEM

London is not
really or surreally
"the place"
and foggy yet
due to
an awful
"although"
it was the place
where our lashing tongue
love almost came crashing down
around our pink and brown
in love heads

London is not the swinging place
for the interracial newly weds

GOOD GLORY

to Hoyt Fuller, editor

IF   HE
SAID OF ME
".....AS FREE AS A MAN
IS LIKELY   TO BE....."
THEN TAKE NOTE YALL
MY CHOSEN ONES /MY CLOSE ONES
MY COMPANIONS /MY FRIENDS
I DO NOT
ALLOW THE TERRORS
OF UNCERTAINESS /PRECARIOUSNESS /
AND INFERIORITY
TO LATCH ON TO ME
HANG ME UP
MAKE ME CRY
IF HE
SAID   THAT OF ME
".....AS FREE AS A MAN
IS LIKELY TO BE....."
THEN WHY SHOULD I
MAKE HIM SEEM   TO LIE?
A M E R I C A ?

I ASK HARLEM

Harlem they say youre a raggidy slave gal   Harlem they
    say

Harlem they say you're a big strong hustling sweaty pal
                Harlem they say

Harlem you've been robed, worked, torndown, and jerked
                al-most to death!

When Whitey used to get his difficult hard-on-to-you Harlem

Then they called you 'the city within a city' filled with
                unfortunates whom nobody cared
                or pitied Ol' Harlem

Harlem you will survive remain alive & creatively arrive
                in spite of white renewal or
                previewed renovations

Harlem you said 'Gimme dat wine', 'Hey-baba-rebop',
                'Sock it to me', and Stomped at
                the Savoy' while shouting
                'BLACK POWER'

You Harlem, I ask you Harlem, to say it loud:
                HARLEM IS BLACK and I'm proud

Say it loud: 'HARLEM IS BLACK and I'm proud' 'HARLEM'S

BLACK and I'm proud'

A COLD

WHY   'BAD' COLD
WHY NOT SAY 'GLAD' COLD
WHY NOT, BETTER STILL 'A GOOD COLD'
WHY NOT, YET IF YOU WILL, FOR A BEST DESCRIP-
    TION OF YOUR MISERABLE CONDITION
                    SAY: 'I HAVE A WHITE COLD!'

MAU MAU MESSAGE TO LIBERALS

IF YOU AINT THE ENEMY
ALTHOUGH YOU LOOK LIKE THE ENEMY
WORK ALONG SIDE THE ENEMY
AND SOME OF YOUR RELATIVES ARE ENEMY
AND YOUR ENEMY FRIENDS WITH THEIR BLATANT
ENEMY POSITIONS   DOING EVERYDAY
ENEMY ACTIONS   TO   US
DO NOT ATTACK SISTER SOUL AND BROTHER BLACK
BECAUSE THEY HATE AND BATTLE THE ENEMY
THAT ENEMY THAT LOOKS LIKE YOU
WHOM DAILY RIDES THEIR ENSLAVED   BLACK BACKS

IT ALL DEPENDS

What are
white
women
between the
sad/bad
tried & tired
ages
made of........?

meat & bone
in heavy masses
or tubercular
bitches
with flat asses

what are
they made out of.....?

money first
& madness last
cigarette tar
smiles that
scar
hair spray
to make stringy hair stay
hair dye
to be young or look-a-lie
cold cream
to be something they seem
makeup base
trying to mask a mental ugly face
rouge/powder/eye shadow/eye liner/
false eyelashes/ and tons of tube lipstick
(they loud talk so much
their lips never do get stuck
it would be great if   they would lipstick
but no luck)
nail polish/false nails/hand lotion
and any other gimmick
that is commercially set in motion

they buy these lies
on a whim or notion
what falsities
that white
women paint on/paste on/strap on/pin on/
and mentally or physically (or both)
depend upon
could fill an awesome unnatural ocean

so what
black
women
between the
white fashions
and natural sensations
want to give tribute
to made up women
by the art
of imitation?

ENTRAILS

Insomuch that you will not ever.....
Insomuch that you will never.......
Insomuch that you would rather.....
    cry barrels of blood
    bleed plastic bags of snot
vomit various piles of
undigested artificial
foods   fill the forests of vast valleys
with bowel filth   join rectums! defecate rivelets for
mangy pink rats to bath their diseased offsprings in
Inasmuch that these hideous offerings are now
    advertised on War Street Shock Change
    'ALL THE FILTH FIT TO FART!' (all the evil rot to
    destroy
    the heart) Insomuch that you refuse nature/the natural/
    the fresh/the primitive/proven spiritual fact   I offer
you this America   this man-made entrail attack

U.S. CITY TITTY

to James Forman

WHITE CITY WITH BLACK SHADOWS
BOTH GOING CRAZY TOGETHER
BLACK CITY WITH WHITE SHADOWS
BOTH G O N E   CRAZY   A P A R T

THE CORRECT WORD

The correct word
at the correct time
calculated to explode
inside of the target's brain
is the right way
to write/read/or recite
revolutionary poetry

THE SAX BIT

This poem is
just a poem of
thanks

This bent metal serpent/ holy horn with lids like beer
mug/ with phallic tail   why did they invent you
before Coleman Hawkins   was   born   ?
This curved shiney tune gut/ hanging lynched like/ J
shaped initial of jazz / wordless without a reed   when
Coleman Hawkins first fondled it/kissed it with Black
sound   did Congo blood sucking Belges frown   ?
This tenor/alto/bass/baritone/soprano/moan/cry &
shout-a-phone !   sex-oh-phone/tell-it-like-damn-
sho-isa-phone !What tremors ran through Adolphe
Saxe the day Bean grabbed his   ax ?
This golden mine of a million marvelous sounds/black
notes with myriad shadows/or empty crooked tube of
technical white poor-formance/calculated keys that
never unlock soul doors/white man made machine saved
from zero   by Coleman Hawkins !
This saxophone salvation/modern gri gri hanging from
jazzmen's necks   placed there   by Coleman Hawkins
a full body & soul sorcerer whose spirit dwells eternally
in every saxophone NOW and all those   sound-a-phones
to be

THE 'LEFT-OVERS' OF EUROPE

HERE   OVERTHERE   WHERE   THEY USED TO SEND
DOUGHBOYS   THOSE 'FARTING 69 SOLJEERS'   HERE
NOW 1969   THEY HAVE   MORE DOUGH   THAN
BAKERIES AND BANKS
EUROPE AGAIN   STRIVING UP   THEIR IMPERIALISTIC
WHITE-ONLY   TOP TEN   LADDER   PUTTING DOWN
THE USA   EVERY STEP   OF THEIR   UPWARD
NEO-COLONIALISTS WAY   UPWARD THEY CLIMB
ROBBING AND REELING   PROMISES   TOKENS   WHILE
THEY CONTINUE STEALING   CRYING CROCODILE NATO
MONSOON   TEARS   FOR VIETNAM   PRETENDING
TO WORK TOWARDS ITS ENDING   THUS OFFENDING
THEIR RICH SAVIOR   UNCLE   SAM   BUT FAIL TO
BLOW UP   OR DOWN   ONE AMERICAN EXPRESSES
IN MEMORY   OF FOUR BLACK   CHILDREN   MURDERED
IN ALABAM   SUNDAY SCHOOL DRESSES
EUROPE'S   YOUTH   GETS   HEADLINES GALORE
AND YET   NOT ONE   HAS FIRED A REVOLUTIONARY
GUN   AT THEIR   WELL KNOWN   ENEMY   NOT EVEN
FOR FUN   BUT THEY DO BUY   AMERICAN FLAGS   TO
BURN   (WHEN WILL EUROPEAN ACTIVIST LEFT LEARN)
NO   BODY   OF THE USA   CARES IF EUROPEANS
BURN   A FLAG   A DAY   WHAT   THOSE LEFT-OVERS
GOT TO DO   IS SET FIRE   TO A TOURIST   AMERICAN
JUST LIKE YOU!

SURREALLY HUNGRY

Black eyed peas big as elephants
pinto beans bright as diamonds
rice raining from the skies
biscuits soft as clouds
I sat upside up on an overturned pancake wondering were
U.S. whites white and proud
did they say it loud - out loud?

Black eyed peas spying across a womb
pinto beans exploding under a broom
rice racing over a locked door's transom
I sat downward down wondering did
U.S. whites call themselves tall, dark, and handsome
If they did so : are turtles chitterling
or double breasted tit beaters?

SKY HIGH

New York
(New Amsterdam)
your tall
cold grey
buildings
are still
scraping sky
tell us
why
do they
represent
tombstones
to be
lived in
when
roses dont
rise
very high
toward
a scraped
sky
in New
Manhattan
where
plastics
replaced
silks and
serious
Old Amsterdam satin

PAN AFRICAN

dedicated to Kwame Nkrumah

While all Africa is here in the sun
Those African creative workers
And those of the gun
LET'S UNITE OUR EFFORTS / AS ONE!

To free every African
To Free every African
To free every African
To Free every African
To FRREEEE every African
To FREEEEEEEE every African
To FREEEEEEEEEEEEE every African

Let's unite our forces as one
Let's attack with African power
Let's unite as one   unite as one
Let's attack with African Power
AND GET THE JOB DONE!!!

MAHALIA JACKSON

Mahalia Jackson   blackdignity   big VOICE big SOUL
  encased in a BIG warm body   clad in splendor clothing
  the best of the best   glad rags of the West
   Mahalia Jackson   piano & organ to anchor her song down
    beautiful woman hands clasped in prayer   eyes closed
    to despair
     Mahalia Jackson mouth soft with song   and voice range
    true
      Congo on stage in Brooklyn!
Afro America's spirit mother   Just A Close Of
 Walk With Thee   Granted!! Let it be! Black Power Yes
  Lord Let it be! Mahalia Jackson Billie Holiday, Bessie
  Smith...! and that unknown mother taken in slavery
  as she screamed on the auction block when Whitey
  snatched
   her only baby away   Mahalia Jackson greater than all
   her dignified humbleness always doing her best
    big mama of song spreading unrealized rumours of
    Christianity   doing no wrong   Mahalia Jackson on
    stage in a white low keyed light   Congo caught on in
    Brooklyn this night

GOD BLAME AMERICA!!

America/Miss America is over paid, over fed, over
    stuffed and now over here!
America/poets   dont fasten their flies no more
America/shoes can not be worn out on fingers
America/Germany is just as strong as America under arms
America/Mickey the Mouse is colored
America/whiskey contains cigarette cancer
America/I lick stamps on the wrong side
America/nine to five aint forever, is it?
America/your fliptop box is showing
America/your women sound like sex starved Donald Ducks
America/the electric chair is too comfortable for your
    officials
America/I do not want to be integrated into you
America/I continue eating watermelons on TV for a fee
America/Why do I scare thee when I attempt to live free?
America/hot dogs cant be hamburgers much longer
America/Jazz has won the youth of the world
America/rhinoceroses are lonely in the zoos
America/the ghosts of Indians haunt your family nightly?
America/many of them aint really ready, are they?
America/Kosher cats closed my contract to you
America/screaming is still valid
America/I do believe you're afraid
America/Munchen maids dance black
America/I sing Round Bout Midnight
America/Your eyes are nervous
America/your handshake's a fake
America/your mask has slipped
America/your whites arent hip
America/their blues aint sad
America/your image is bad
America/surrender to the East! Forget the West! Go it
    alone, that's best!
America can you hear me? America, did you hear what I
    said? America??
    (a voice) FUCK YOU!
America/MAY I?

AN AFFAIR

MONEY MADE

LOVE

TO AMERICA

AMERICA

MARRIED MONEY

AT FIRST BITE

EARLY MORNING WARNING POEM

a bright spring day   the dew drop dawn sleeps now   the
birds of all feathers frolic   roosters crow suddenly
shutters on windows open now   flowers salute the sun
warm beams kiss the early earth   trees yawn lofty good
mornings now   fields of lazy oats wave hello world   a
dead lonely leaf falls to the ground   a young lamb baas for
breakfast near the red rose bush
ME   MACHINE GUN   GRENADES   camouflaged in
America suburbia with out CAR FARE   LIBERATION
FOR MY PEOPLE   GUERILLA WAR FARE

HARLEM POSTER

IN A POST OFFICE
WHERE ONE BUYS STAMPS
LICKS THEM
STICKS THEM
ON HASTY IMPORTANT LETTERS
AND UNIMPORTANT CARDS
THEY HAD PASTED
A "WANTED" POSTER
WHERE   NOTICES
FOR OPPORTUNITIES/JOBS/ETC
WERE   DISPLAYED
THIS "WANTED" POSTER
STUCK THERE
PINNED THERE
AMONGST GOVERNMENT OPENINGS
WAS AN F.B.I.
LAW   AND   ORDER   LIE
FOR   A   REVOLUTIONARY
BROTHER
AS   INNOCENT
AS   I

NO MO SPACE FOR TOMS

there out there in the underspace
is a lake of octaves
lunar keys float out there in the
direction of harmonies
Heard only by listeners
with ears of years of Zanzibars
legions of listeners out there
empty pockets of space
is nothing more than devoured cornbread
Dedan Mikathi drove a Mau Mau train
drove a Mau Mau train to victory
there out there in British East
is a musical moon of mountains
revolutionary keys that unlock
chains swifter than Cuban rum
tribal dance of harmony harambee
heard and heeded by guerillas
with astra-cosmo tomorrows as Sun Ra
an arkestra filled to the brim
with sounds of vegetables
columns of almost extinct colonialists
entangled in tarantula webs of greed
green back mambas strangle them
there out there in the otherspace
is the lakes of octobers
deeper than distance
traveled Tom time blasted away

a tear of sadness shed by the West
to a vest pocket Tom he was

ANSWERS

the reasons are as numerous as leaves on the pavement
the cause is as plentiful as wet in a drop of water
the whys are as bright as eyes of an African baby
the wheres are as obvious as a church on Easter
the whens come around fast as sister of time
the how it will be done is the secret surprise
the who is me and the who is you
the what is, what for,
the what to do
is the
spiritual action between me and guilty you!

EN GARDE!

to Archie Shepp

They are banning together   they are setting things   aside
    for themselves
They are looking out   only   for themselves
They build destructive weapons together
and   the Third World knows   who 'they' are

They are sinking   together
They are stinking up the entire world
They are denying human rights   to all non-whites
They bring death   with their promises
and the Third World watches who 'they' hire

They are screaming about 'population explosion'
They have built bigger bombs   to cut us down
They are wearing a face of guilt and alcoholic frowns
They wave dollars across the troubled sky
thus the Third World rises, EN GARDE!!
and the Third World of action makes them die
en garde! my rainbow colored brothers! en garde! soul
    brothers! en garde!

SOUL ON THE LAM

Well brother C   whose expensive book   I aint yet read
whose image I aint seen   those fay fathers of this
un-united states have united   to keep their   appointed
NATIONAL   NIGGER   NUISANCE   in place   they have
forced you to go on the run   they hunt you now   with
international computer   and ghetto Uncle Tommy gun
they thought that you brother E.C. could be over publicized
and bought easily   but you fooled their 'ramparts red
blare'   and spread Black T.C.B. everywhere   now they
want your hide   causing you to hide   in and out side of
the scene   At your cocktail party   nearly all was white
and only one Panther unleashed that night   thats when you
ran
ran   for real (?) President   or just publicity time well
spent   but looking back   and thinking hard twice
arent these the same whitefolks that put   your   soul   on
ice?

BLACK REPEATER

dedicated to all my children in what land they may be

REMEMBER THIS   REMEMBER THAT   AND DONT
     FORGET
THAT YOURE BLACK!
FORGET THIS   FORGET THAT   AND ALWAYS
     REMEMBER
THAT YOURE BLACK
          (repeat as many times as necessary)

BRAINS

They are killing all the good guys
what kind of movie is this?
preachers/presidents/prime ministers/heroes/and even
    some of their own
They are shooting all the good guys
in the head   in their heads   Bang! BANG!!
Because those who murder   or have them assassinated
are afraid of their brains
They are killing all the good guys
What kind of movie is this?

ONE BLUE NOTE

when I was almost
nine months unborn
inside the belly
under the breast
under the maternity dress
inside the vaginal cave
doubled up womb deep
inside my daddy's wife
his steady laymate
    his chick, his love life
    my mother
it was then I first knew
Jazz was a black classical music
that is created each time one blew TRUE

BLACK TALENT

Yes he is good
damn good and talented
and all yall knows it !
So...dont let him have to go to....
dont allow him to starve and.......
dont force him to.........
dont make him ask them for.......
dont ignore him until they turn you onto him

> He's a Black talent/yours !
> he yearns for your support
> He yearns to earn from
> Black folks his own folks
> Help is what he pleads and needs!
> Cant you rich negroes????

POEM WHY

what is a poem
when a man is not free
when a child cant eat
when a woman cant bear fruit
when fear and death lurk in the streets

what is a poem then

it is a sharp bolt of
   lightening that frees man
it is a bowlful of red beans
   and rice in rhyme   for child
it is bouquet of praises
   that seduces and enchants
   a woman until she blossoms forth
The poet's poem power prowls
   through the nasty neon streets
   demystifying death
   and replacing fear with courage
that is what a poem is
when the men arent free
when children cant eat
when women cant bear fruit
and when fear and death
   lurk in streets
that is the <u>what</u>
that is the poem <u>why</u>

SIGNATURE is a new series of shorter works, distinguished by the highly personal and imaginative approach of the author to his subject. It comprises works of poetry and prose, fiction and non-fiction, and includes English, American, and translated texts.